LAR
TOMC.

Personal Evangelism

FRONTIER PUBLISHING INTERNATIONAL
in association with
WORD PUBLISHING

Word (UK) Ltd
Milton Keynes, England

WORD AUSTRALIA
Kilsyth, Victoria, Australia

WORD COMMUNICATIONS LTD
Vancouver, B.C., Canada

STRUIK CHRISTIAN BOOKS (PTY) LTD
Maitland, South Africa

CHRISTIAN MARKETING NEW ZEALAND LTD
Havelock North, New Zealand

JENSCO LTD
Hong Kong

JOINT DISTRIBUTORS SINGAPORE –
ALBY COMMERCIAL ENTERPRISES PTE LTD
and
CAMPUS CRUSADE

SALVATION BOOK CENTRE
Malaysia

PERSONAL EVANGELISM

© Larry Tomczak 1992

Published by Frontier Publishing International in association with Word Publishing.

ISBN 0-85009-800-9 (Australia 1-86258-213-0)

Unless otherwise indicated, Scripture quotations are from the New International Version (NIV), © 1973, 1978, 1984 by International Bible Society.
Other Scripture quotations are from the following sources:
The New American Standard Bible (NASB), © 1960, 1962, 1963, 1968, 1971, 1972, 1973, 1975, 1977 the Lockman Foundation.
The Authorised Version of the Bible (AV).
The Revised Standard Version (RSV), copyright © 1971 by Division of Christian Education of the National Council of Churches of Christ in the United States of America.

The quotations in the following studies are all used by permission.

Studies 1,7,9,10,11,13,21,24,27 from *Effective Evangelism*, by J. Oswald Sanders, © 1982, STL Productions, Kingstown Broadway, Carlisle.
Studies 2,31 from *The ABC of Personal Evangelism*, by Ron Smith, © 1964, STL Productions.
Study 3 from *Divine Appointments*, by Larry Tomczak, © 1986 Larry Tomczak, Servant Publications, Box 8617, Ann Arbor, Michigan 48107.
Studies 6,14,18 from *14,000 Quips & Quotes*, by E. C. McKenzie, © 1991, Baker Book House, Grand Rapids, Michigan.
Studies 8,19,25,26,27,28,29 from *Great Quotes and Illustrations*, compiled by George Sweeting, © 1985, Word Books, 9 Holdom Avenue, Bletchley, Milton Keynes, MK1 1QR.
Studies 12,16 from *Everyday Evangelism*, by Billie Hanks Jr., © 1986, Word Books.
Studies 15, 23 from *Day by Day with C. H. Spurgeon*, compiled by Al Bryant, © 1985, Word Books.
Study 20 from *My God is Real*, by David Watson, © David Watson 1970, Kingsway Publications, Eastbourne.

Reproduced, printed and bound in Great Britain by BPCC Hazells Ltd., member of BPCC Ltd.

92 93 94 95 / 10 9 8 7 6 5 4 3 2 1

Making the most of the studies ...

Welcome to the Oasis study on *Personal Evangelism!* The book has been written with the goal of *helping you to become more effective in sharing your faith.* You will find it informative, practical and inspiring. We suggest that you take two days to cover each study and therefore two months to complete the book. You might want to work through the material more quickly, but if you take your time you are likely to benefit more. We recommend that you use the New International Version of the Bible (post-1983 version).

Grow in knowledge and confidence

Personal evangelism needn't be a struggle when it can be an adventure. Larry Tomczak bridges the gap and shows us how we can actually enjoy sharing our faith.

He understands the battles that many of us go through, and often gives examples of his own personal experiences — some of which are extremely humorous! He approaches the subject of evangelism in a particularly refreshing way.

The three sections under the main text relate to the teaching material. You may be asked to consider some aspect of evangelism, to write down an answer, or to do something practical. The questions have been designed to challenge you about the needs of the unsaved and to help you to discover how you can reach out to them. Let the Scripture verses encourage you to consider how God feels about personal evangelism.

Build a storehouse

The Bible says, 'Wise men store up knowledge' (Prov. 10:14), and Jesus encourages us to '[bring] good things out of the good stored up in [our] heart' (Luke 6:45).

The 'Food for thought' section gives you the invaluable opportunity of hearing from God direct and of storing up what He says to you. **Please use a separate notebook** particularly for this section. It will help you to crystallise your thoughts, and it will also be of tremendous reference value in the future.

Pray that God will speak to you. You may find that you're so enthralled by what He says to you that you're looking up many Scriptures which are not even suggested!

In studies 20 to 28, 'Food for thought' has been replaced by 'Action point', since the studies lend themselves to role-play and Scripture memorisation.

Finally, may God help you to understand that you have a vital part to play in reaching the world for Jesus. And may He encourage you as you take practical steps to make Him known.

I'm afraid

God did not give us a spirit of timidity, but a spirit of power, of love and of self-discipline (2 Tim. 1:7).

Gird your sword upon your side, O mighty one ... In your majesty ride forth victoriously on behalf of truth (Ps. 45:3,4a).

There is no mention in Scripture of Timothy's father. Maybe he died early, leaving his son without a strong image of manhood to follow. Maybe Timothy's stomach problems resulted from his being nervous. We don't know. What we do know is that Timothy wept. He needed to be exhorted to 'fan into flame the gift of God' and 'not be ashamed to testify about our Lord' (2 Tim. 1:6,8).

When it comes to evangelism, how many of us can identify with Timothy? We look at the terrible needs around us and know that we have the answer to them. Yet when it comes to sharing Jesus, we are overcome with fear.

'Look at people with other beliefs,' we are told. 'They're not afraid. The Communists caught Lenin's vision and marched with it for over seventy years. The Muslims are believing for world takeover and are recruiting vast numbers for their cause. The Mormons and Jehovah's Witnesses are continually on our doorsteps, handing out their literature, preaching their message. The counterfeit gospel is advancing. What's happening to the truth?'

We hear these things and guilt is added to fear. We think of the people we know who have

▓ **To consider**

Are you fearful of anything? Nail your fears by writing them down.

_____

_____

_____

God has the solution. Seek Him for it.

▓ **To meditate on**

God wants you to overcome fear.
'Do not be afraid, little flock, for your Father has been pleased to give you the kingdom' (Luke 12:32).
'Say to those with fearful hearts, "Be strong, do not fear; your God will come"' (Isa. 35:4a).
'The LORD is my light and my salvation — whom shall I fear? The LORD is the stronghold of my life — of whom shall I be afraid?' (Ps. 27:1).

never become Christians: that son who's rejected his religious upbringing; those parents who are pew-fillers; that girl who's just had an abortion; those friends who seem indifferent to spiritual things. 'I really want to share the gospel with them,' we say, 'but I can't.'

Today the Lord Jesus is preparing His people for a great awakening and for the ultimate restoration of His church. He is calling us to overcome our 'spirit of timidity' because He has given us His 'spirit of power' (2 Tim. 1:7). He doesn't want us to be grovelling in fear and guilt over the unsaved. He wants us to be marching confidently, an evangelistic people who are zealous for the advance of His kingdom and effective in their day-to-day witness. He is looking for a church which does not see evangelism as 'the theme for the month' but as a lifestyle.

One day every knee will bow to Jesus. We have been given a commission: to reach the world for Him before He returns. God wants to involve you in it. He wants to shake you out of your past failures, give you His heart for the lost and equip you to share the gospel more effectively. Welcome to the adventure!

▨ To encourage

Read Exodus 4:10–12.

Did God hear what Moses said? YES/NO

Write out and memorise verse 12.

_____

_____

_____

> What does it mean to fear the Lord?

> In a concordance find references to the fear of the Lord in the Psalms.

> What will be the benefits for those who fear Him? (e.g. God confides in them and makes His covenant known to them — Ps. 25:14).

In days when capital punishment was current, a chaplain escorted Charles Peace, a notorious criminal, to the scaffold. He was a forger, a burglar, a double murderer. As they walked, the chaplain endeavoured to extend to him 'the consolations of religion'. As he spoke of Christ's power to save, the condemned man turned to him saying, 'Do you believe it? Do you believe it? If I believed that, I would willingly crawl across England on broken glass to tell men it was true.'
J. Oswald Sanders

Why don't we evangelise?

I tell you, now is the time of God's favour, now is the day of salvation (2 Cor. 6:2b).

Godly sorrow brings repentance that leads to salvation and leaves no regret, but worldly sorrow brings death (2 Cor. 7:10).

Before we can receive fresh teaching we often need to uproot old beliefs. Why do many of us shy away from sharing our faith?

Procrastination. Procrastination means 'putting off until tomorrow what you have already put off until today'. Many Christians know that they are supposed to be evangelising but simply haven't got around to it. The disciples seem to have had this problem. Jesus rebuked them for saying, 'Four months more and then the harvest.' He said, 'I tell you, open your eyes and look at the fields! They are ripe for harvest' (John 4:35).

Discouragement. Some of us may be discouraged by shallow results from past evangelistic endeavours. We have heard people preach a sugar-coated gospel. 'Just make a decision for Jesus,' they say. But they place no emphasis on repentance or the Lordship of Christ. Jesus told us to make disciples, not decisions. As we watch individuals drift away from the church, our zeal for continued evangelistic activity dwindles and threatens to die altogether.

Spectator mentality. Many believers see evangelism as a specialised ministry for those

▓ To consider

How would you sum up your attitude to evangelism?

_____

_____

What is God saying to you about it?

_____

▓ To meditate on

God wants you to live for His glory.
'It is written: "I believed; therefore I have spoken." With that same spirit of faith we also believe and therefore speak' (2 Cor. 4:13).
'We cannot help speaking about what we have seen and heard' (Acts 4:20).
'Let your light shine before men, that they may see your good deeds and praise your Father in heaven' (Matt. 5:16).

with a unique gift and calling. 'Jesus said that we must be witnesses, not do witnessing,' they say. 'We ordinary Christians just let our light shine. I share Jesus with people who come up to me asking what's different about my life. But I don't go out of my way to talk about Him.'

Clearly not all of us have the ministry gift of evangelism but we are all called to 'do the work of an evangelist' (2 Tim. 4:5) as the Spirit leads us. That is the example of the New Testament church where you never find silent witnesses. The early believers shared the gospel wherever they went.

Two men worked together for years then one of them was born again. When he told his friend he was informed, 'I've been a Christian for ages. Didn't you know?' The new believer replied, 'You're the main reason why I haven't become a Christian. I thought that if people were as good as you they wouldn't need God.'

Certainly, the way we live is meant to witness to the grace and power of God, but demonstration without proclamation is insufficient. If you work well and say nothing, you will be seen as a nice person and absorb the glory that should be given to Jesus.

▨ To pray

Write down the names of any work colleagues or close friends who are not aware you're a Christian.

_____

_____

_____

Pray for opportunities to share Jesus with them.

➤ If someone started giving you excuses why he needn't witness, what Scriptures would you share with him? Write them down.

_____

_____

_____

_____

_____

Every Christian should be a witness. Grace is shown to a Christian in order that he might reflect it to others. He is granted light that he might show others the way: truth, that he might be a guide to those yet in darkness: life, that others seeing that life in him might desire it too! Christian! You have been given all these things — grace, light, truth and life. You have received Christ — your whole desire should now be — 'Lord, use me — even me in reaching some lost one for Thee'.
Ron Smith

Why don't we evangelise?

For I resolved to know nothing while I was with you except Jesus Christ and him crucified (1 Cor. 2:2).

For I have not hesitated to proclaim to you the whole will of God (Acts 20:27).

More reasons why people are not evangelising:

Bad experiences. Our enthusiasm for evangelism may have been dampened by gimmicks or poor presentations that lack spiritual power and reality. Alternatively, we may have been put off because we have seen some dreadful evangelistic attempts by others.

Saturation. Preachers are meant to equip the saints in every area of their lives, not to prepare a saturation diet of one main topic. Sadly, many Christians have come from a church background where evangelism was preached at almost every meeting. Like people who eat too much of one good thing, they feel sick. Later, they join a different church but whenever the challenge comes to evangelise, they switch off.

Weariness. Some Christians were once on fire for Jesus. They were involved in frenzied evangelistic activities, bombarding people with Scriptures and sharing their faith in rather a tactless way. Now the fire has gone out and the devil has taken them to the opposite extreme — passivity. Today they're almost indifferent about evangelism, and they give themselves excuses

▓ **To consider**

Which of the above reasons not to evangelise is a problem for you?

_____

_____

How are you going to overcome them?

_____

_____

▓ **To meditate on**

God wants you to persevere.
'Consider him who endured such opposition from sinful men, so that you will not grow weary and lose heart'
(Heb. 12:3).
'I will build my church, and the gates of Hades will not overcome it'
(Matt. 16:18b).
'Go and make disciples of all nations'
(Matt. 28:19).

as to why they shouldn't be involved in it.

Cosiness. Sometimes believers so enjoy one another's company that they slowly lose the vision for evangelism and develop a theology to justify abandoning outreach. 'Small is beautiful,' they say. 'We're after quality, not quantity. After all, Jesus did say, "Where two or three are gathered together ..." ' They feel threatened by anything that might break up their 'holy huddle'.

Imbalance. 'These days God is emphasising building the church,' say some believers. 'We can't evangelise until we're mature enough.' They look at their nice, orderly housegroups and imagine the chaos there would be if a load of new converts descended on them. In this way they focus on pastoral care and escape their responsibility to the unsaved.

But building the church is only half the story.

The heartbeat of the Father is this: reach the church and reach the world.

We must run on both tracks — community and evangelism. So while Spirit-led planning, discipling and leadership training are vital, we must give equal commitment to the lost.

▓ To question

What do you think about the quote by Stephen Olford on this page?

_____

_____

How can believers be motivated to evangelise?

_____

➤ In a dictionary find the definition of the word 'witness'.

➤ Look up these references about our being God's witnesses: Isa. 43:10; 44:8; Luke 24:48; Acts 1:8; 2:32; 3:15; 10:41; 13:31; 26:22.

It is characteristic of our natural sluggishness and laziness to put off the work of evangelism. By cunning calculations and clever rationalizations, we talk ourselves out of the urgency of the task and the demand upon our time, talents, and treasures. How we need to ask the Holy Spirit to rid us of all unbelief, indifference, prejudice, and hard-heartedness.
Stephen Olford

Why don't we evangelise?

Pride goes before destruction, a haughty spirit before a fall (Prov. 16:18).

A man's pride brings him low, but a man of lowly spirit gains honour (Prov. 29:23).

For what other reasons are we reluctant to evangelise?

Pride. Many people wrongly think, 'Oh, evangelism? That's elementary stuff. I'm moving into the deep things of God: church concepts, restoration, apostolic ministry and so on. Evangelism is for the enthusiastic new converts. Let's send them out.' The happiest place in a hospital is the maternity unit. People do some funny things there and get away with it. Nothing shakes the sophistication out of a church like brand-new converts.

A guy came to the Lord one Friday night. He was fresh out of the disco scene and turned up at the Sunday meeting. The worship leader said, 'Let's praise the Lord!' and this guy did a boogie across the floor declaring, 'Right on, baby! Praise ya, Jesus!' His action was met with critical and judgemental stares — until someone shared publicly that he had come to Christ only hours before. Then these fossilised Christians were jolted out of their sophistication! The young man's background was a mess, and his language was raw, but his love for Jesus was real. You could almost see conviction creeping over the congregation.

▓ To discover

Which of your natural abilities or disabilities can get in the way of the Spirit?
abilities: intellectual achievements ...

_____

disabilities: shyness ...

_____

Ask God to help you to overcome them.

▓ To meditate on

God calls you to be humble.
'He humbled himself and became obedient to death — even death on a cross!' (Phil. 2:8)
'Therefore, whoever humbles himself like this child is the greatest in the kingdom of heaven' (Matt. 18:4).
'Humble yourselves, therefore, under God's mighty hand, that he may lift you up in due time' (1 Pet. 5:6).

We say, 'I'm on a quest for deeper wisdom.'
God says, 'You're too respectable. You've lost
your radical edge, your sense of reckless
abandonment, your enthusiasm and love for
Me.' Evangelism is not just for the few gifted
believers or the new converts. It's for everyone.

Lack of power. Jesus told His disciples, 'You
will receive power when the Holy Spirit comes
on you; and you will be my witnesses' (Acts
1:8). Some believers have never received the
baptism in the Spirit and need to seek it.
Others depend too much on their own natural
abilities when they should rely on the Spirit.

Lack of instruction. Many Christians are
shy about sharing their faith because they have
never really been taught by someone who has
the gift of evangelist (Eph. 4:11). We have an
Evangelism Training School. One day we teach,
then we tell everyone, 'Right, we're going to put
it into practice tomorrow.' The next day they're
battling with questions like, 'What about the
heathen?' or 'How do you know Jesus rose from
the dead?' When they get back to the
classroom, they're desperate to know how to
reply. I pray that these notes will give you the
answers you need to be more effective.

➤ If someone said to you, 'I want to know more about the baptism in the Holy Spirit,' what Scriptures would you show him? Write them down for future reference.

_____

_____

_____

_____

▓ To confess

Be honest with yourself and repent of any ways in
which you have excused yourself from sharing the
gospel.

Pray now that God will begin to give you fresh
opportunities to speak for Him.

I hear, I forget.
I see, I remember.
I do, I understand.
Chinese proverb

Called to evangelise

'Therefore go and
make disciples of all
nations' (Matt. 28:19).

'Go into all the world
and preach the good
news to all creation'
(Mark 16:15).

'Repentance and
forgiveness of sins will
be preached in his
name to all nations'
(Luke 24:47a).

'As the Father has sent
me, I am sending you'
(John 20:21).

The Great Commission is not the Great Suggestion. Evangelism is not an option. To every Christian Jesus says, not only, 'Come to me,' but also, 'Go into all the world.' The original command, 'Be fruitful and increase in number' (Gen. 1:28) which was directed to the human race now becomes the mandate for God's people, 'I chose ... you to go and bear fruit' (John 15:16). All four gospels end with the theme of evangelism, and the book of Acts carries on that theme. 'But you will receive power when the Holy Spirit comes on you; and you will be my witnesses ... to the ends of the earth' (Acts 1:8).

The Bible tells us, 'there is ... no one who seeks God' (Rom. 3:11). That's why Jesus came — not just to save the lost, but to seek them too (Luke 19:10). He now says to us, 'Go out into the highways (where people are easier to reach) and along the hedges (where you've got to seek for them), and compel them to come in' (Luke 14:23 NASB). (Words in brackets are mine.)

Paul was obsessed with evangelism. In Romans 1:14–16 he cites three times 'I am ...'.
'I am under obligation' (v.14 NASB).
Evangelism is not for volunteers. God has

▓ To consider

In your opinion, what sort of people are:
'in the highways'?

_____

'along the hedges'?

_____

▓ To meditate on

God wants you to reach the lost.
'Here is a trustworthy saying that deserves full acceptance: Christ Jesus came into the world to save sinners' (1 Tim. 1:15).
'It is not the healthy who need a doctor, but the sick. I have not come to call the righteous, but sinners to repentance' (Luke 5:31,32).

committed to all of us, 'the message of reconciliation. We are therefore Christ's ambassadors, as though God were making his appeal through us' (2 Cor. 5:19b,20). 'Woe to me if I do not preach the gospel!' (1 Cor. 9:16b).

'I am eager to preach the gospel' (v.15 NASB). God doesn't want us to view evangelism like unpleasant medicine — to be taken when absolutely necessary. Evangelism is not a chore, it's an adventure. God wants us to be enthusiastic about it — compelled not by duty but by Christ's love (2 Cor. 5:14).

'I am not ashamed of the gospel' (v.16 NASB). Paul refused to be intimidated, apologetic or fearful of people's opinions. He didn't worry when Governor Festus declared, 'You are out of your mind, Paul! ... Your great learning is driving you insane' (Acts 26:24). Paul's attitude was, 'If we are out of our mind, it is for the sake of God' (2 Cor. 5:13a).

You have been called to evangelise. Don't give in to fear and don't let discouragement slow you down. God is eager to see you play your part in reaching this world for Jesus.

➤ In a dictionary look up the meaning of the words 'reconcile' and 'ambassador' and write them down.

_____

_____

_____

_____

➤ Meditate on the following verses which underline Christ's work of reconciliation and our responsibility as His ambassadors: Rom. 5:10; 2 Cor. 5:16–20; Eph. 2:16; Col. 1:20.

▨ To do

How, in practical ways, can we reach:
the 'highway' people?

_____

the 'hedge' people?

_____

What are you doing?

_____

No one ever followed Jesus who didn't become a fisher of men. If you're not fishing, it's questionable how closely you're following!
Dawson Trotman (founder of the Navigators)
Used by permission of the Navigators, USA.

Bring and build

'Go up into the mountains and bring down timber and build the house, so that I may take pleasure in it and be honoured' (Hag. 1:8).

'My house ... remains a ruin, while each of you is busy with his own house' (Hag. 1:9b).

W hen the Israelites returned from Babylon to Jerusalem they started building the House of the Lord. After a while the work was halted because the people became preoccupied with their own affairs. God's Word through the restoration prophet, Haggai, stirred the remnant to resume the building.

Today God says to us, 'Bring in the lost and build the church.' Evangelism and community are two sides of the same coin.

Sadly, some Christians fall into the same trap as the Israelites — they become preoccupied with self. When they have a problem they focus on it and analyse it. Then they take it to various church leaders and analyse it some more. They are eventually so problem-centred that they become depressed and lose their 'victory mentality' altogether.

When a great persecution broke out against the early church did the believers become self-centred? No. We read, 'all except the apostles were scattered throughout Judea and Samaria ... (and) preached the word wherever they went' (Acts 8:1b,4). The apostles remained in Jerusalem while the believers went out. No one thought, 'Evangelism is this month's

▓ To beware

Beware of imitating the third servant in Matthew 25:14–30.
Why did he hide his talent?

_____

What did the master call this servant?

_____

What did the master call his other two servants?

_____

▓ To meditate on

Jesus wants you to work with Him as He builds His house.
'Now, my son, the LORD be with you, and may you have success and build the house of the LORD your God, as he said you would' (1 Chr. 22:11).
'Let your hands be strong so that the temple may be built' (Zech. 8:9b).
'Go out to the roads and country lanes and make them come in, so that my house will be full' (Luke 14:23).

theme, then we'll move on to something else.'
For everyone, evangelism was a way of life.

In this day of restoration God is calling His
people to abandon self-centredness, apathy and
indifference. He doesn't want us looking in at
ourselves, declaring smugly, 'We've got our
Christian fellowship. We're being equipped and
set free. We're coming into a greater revelation
of God and finding out who we are in Christ.'

God's Word to His church is 'Go up and ...
bring down timber.' If we are not doing this
God's House will go to ruin and we will become
indifferent and ineffective. Maybe that's already
happened to you. You feel dry in your walk with
God. You've tried in vain to discover the reason.

But the answer to your problem may be that
you're not sharing your faith. I can guarantee
that if you begin to do that, streams of living
water will begin to flow from within you.

So don't let Satan lull you into a state of
apathy when God wants you to go. When you
get up in the morning, quote positive Scriptures
to yourself and allow God to use you during the
day. Your little problems will suddenly seem
very insignificant when you meet people with
worse needs who have no God to help them.

➤ Jude exhorts us,
'build yourselves up in
your most holy faith'
(v.20).

➤ Read Romans 8 and
pick out ten things that
you can declare to
yourself about your
wonderful standing in
Christ, e.g. I am not
under condemnation
(v.1), the Spirit of God
lives in me (v.9).

➤ Write down, in a
notebook, five more
similar verses from other
places in the New
Testament.

➤ When you're in
danger of falling into
self-pity, quote these
verses to yourself and
believe them. Resist the
devil and he will flee
from you.

▨ To consider

When we have personal problems, how can we
avoid becoming self-centred and depressed?

_____

_____

_____

_____

**He who lives for himself
does not have very much
to live for.**

He had compassion

The LORD is gracious and compassionate, slow to anger and rich in love. The LORD is good to all; he has compassion on all he has made (Ps. 145:8,9).

A man with leprosy came to him and begged him on his knees, 'If you are willing, you can make me clean' (Mark 1:40).

We read that when Jesus saw the crowds, 'he had compassion on them' (Matt. 9:36). The Greek word which is translated 'compassion' does not reflect an emotional and somewhat superficial sympathy — 'I feel really sorry for them.' It's far deeper than that. Jesus saw the multitudes like harassed and helpless sheep — confused, directionless, purposeless — and He was profoundly moved by them.

What He felt for the crowds, He felt for individuals. When a leper asked for help, Jesus didn't simply heal him. We read, 'Filled with compassion, Jesus reached out his hand and touched the man' (Mark 1:41a). He performed the miracle not out of duty but out of love.

Jesus could have come to earth and acted without much compassion. He could have felt generally sorry for people and still have met their need for salvation, deliverance, healing and direction. But He chose to carry our sorrows (Isa. 53:4) and to sympathise with our weaknesses (Heb. 4:15). He caught the heart of the Father for the people.

When Jesus approached Jerusalem He could have shaken His fist at it and declared, 'You stubborn people didn't recognise me so you'll

▒ To consider

Write down six Bible characters who lacked compassion (e.g. Pharaoh).

_____

_____

_____

_____

▒ To meditate on

Jesus wants you to feel compassion. 'When Jesus saw her weeping, and the Jews ... also weeping, he was deeply moved in spirit and troubled. "Where have you laid him?" he asked. "Come and see, Lord," they replied. Jesus wept' (John 11:33–35).
'Live in harmony with one another; be sympathetic, love as brothers, be compassionate and humble' (1 Pet. 3:8).

pay for it.' No. We read that when He saw the city, 'he wept over it' (Luke 19:41). He was heartbroken that the Jews refused to recognise their Messiah. He pronounced judgement not through revenge but through tears.

Moses caught God's heart. When he realised that the Israelites had been worshipping the golden calf, he didn't go to the Lord and say, 'Look at what they've done. Now let your wrath fall on them. They deserve it.' He went to the Lord, confessed their sin and pleaded for forgiveness. Then he added, '— but if not, then blot me out of the book you have written' (Exod. 32:32). Moses identified with the people so much that he was willing to sacrifice his own salvation for them.

Paul had the same attitude. When he preached the gospel to his fellow countrymen he was often persecuted. Did he turn on his enemies and call down curses from heaven? No. He said, 'I have great sorrow and unceasing anguish in my heart. For I could wish that I myself were cursed and cut off from Christ for the sake of my brothers' (Rom. 9:2,3). He shared God's compassion. God wants us to share it too.

▓ To do

Write down six ways in which we can express love (e.g. mow our neighbour's lawn, buy a small gift).

_____

_____

_____

Do something like this for someone — if possible, an unbeliever — today or tomorrow.

➤ Read Ezekiel chapter 34.

➤ List the faults of the shepherds of Israel. Write down what God will do for His sheep.

_____

_____

_____

_____

_____

_____

_____

➤ Memorise the verse which currently means the most to you.

The Gospel of a broken heart demands the ministry of bleeding hearts. When our sympathy loses its pang we can no longer be the servants of the passion. We can never heal the needs we do not feel. Tearless hearts can never be heralds of the passion. We must pity if we would redeem. We must bleed if we would be ministers of the saving blood.
D. H. Jowett

Sheep without a shepherd

'But while he was still a long way off, his father saw him and was filled with compassion for him; he ran to his son, threw his arms around him and kissed him' (Luke 15:20).

Beneath the smiling veneer and confident words, people are falling apart. They're empty, lonely and hurting — desperate for a shepherd.

If you're perceptive you'll see the lostness written on their faces. Go into a café and watch the husbands and wives. Often they're not communicating. They're just looking around blankly. Go into the street and observe some of the young people. They're standing around in bizarre fashions. Many are into weird activities because the enemy has manipulated and twisted their minds.

On the corner a couple are arguing. A little child is standing beside them, tears streaming down his cheeks. Mummy and Daddy are splitting up and they're asking him, 'Which of us do you want to go with? You choose.' Can you look at that child and experience nothing of the trauma that's going on in his life?

How many millions are using the television as an escape mechanism? They fear for the future and have nothing to talk about, so they sit glued to the screen and block out reality.

Do we block out reality? While Satan releases all the demons that he can, do we muse

▓ To question

What do you think are the reasons for lack of compassion in our hearts?

_____

_____

_____

▓ To meditate on

God wants you to be open-hearted. 'He looked round at them in anger and, deeply distressed at their stubborn hearts, said to the man, "Stretch out your hand"' (Mark 3:5).
'The sacrifices of God are a broken spirit; a broken and contrite heart, O God, you will not despise' (Ps. 51:17).

complacently, 'Well, I'm sorry for people who aren't saved, but I never was much good at sharing the gospel'? Is that the compassion of Jesus coming through? Does that response reflect the Father's heart?

> ➤ Read through the book of Lamentations and underline the verses that reflect Jeremiah's compassion for his people.

This is not a time to be preoccupied with our own little world. It's a time for urgency, for war! Paul was not passive. Almost everywhere he went there was either a revival or a riot!

Are we going to sit back and declare, 'The time has not yet come for the LORD's house to be built' (Hag. 1:2)? Are we simply going to watch while people of other persuasions deceive the world with a false gospel?

May it never be! God longs to see an army who are marching for His glory, seeing people through His eyes and feeling for them with His heart. He wants us to abandon evangelism by guilt and become motivated by love.

He knows that we cannot work up that love, so He's waiting for us to pray, 'Lord, soften me, break my hardness. Let me feel the pain that you feel when you see lives being crushed, families being torn apart and futures being ruined. Give me your compassion and I will do all I can to seek and to save the lost.'

▓ To pray

If you know that you don't share God's compassion for the lost, take steps to discover it.

Begin crying out to God to melt your heart.

Pray more frequently for the unsaved.

Be prepared to be a channel for God's compassion.

The mass of humanity live lives of quiet desperation.
Henry Thoreau

Motives

'Do not be like the hypocrites, for they love ... to be seen by men' (Matt. 6:5a).

It is true that some preach Christ out of envy and rivalry, but others out of good will. The latter do so in love (Phil. 1:15,16a).

Your name and renown are the desire of our hearts (Isa. 26:8).

Paul said, 'We speak as men approved by God to be entrusted with the gospel. We are not trying to please men but God, who tests our hearts' (1 Thess. 2:4). Many Christians think that they are trying to please God when they're actually seeking to please men.

'I've got to evangelise,' says one. 'The leaders are always telling us to do that so I feel I ought to go along.' For him, evangelism is a legalistic obligation and he feels guilty if he fails to turn up.

Another makes sure that other Christians know how faithful he is at evangelism. He thinks to himself, 'If I do well and start leading people to Christ, I'll get a great reputation. The leaders might even promote me to full-time ministry.'

A third says, 'I'm motivated by the sinner's need. I want to see people saved and sorted out.' There's value in this but it still misses the mark. There is a greater motivation: God's honour.

Paul said, 'Christ's love compels us' (2 Cor. 5:14). When we experience God's love we do not need any external compulsion to witness for Him. The desire to share Jesus wells up from

▓ To consider

Examine your motivation — are you living to please God or to please men?

How do you react when you are overlooked or unfairly treated?

Repent of any selfishness and decide to live for God no matter how others behave towards you.

▓ To meditate on

God wants you to serve Him with the right motivation.
'Man looks at the outward appearance, but the LORD looks at the heart' (1 Sam. 16:7b).
'Nothing in all creation is hidden from God's sight. Everything is uncovered and laid bare before the eyes of him to whom we must give account' (Heb. 4:13).

within. We say, 'Father, I long to express my appreciation to you in this way. My greatest desire is to honour you and bring you joy as you see people won to Jesus Christ.'

Jesus tells us that there is, 'more rejoicing in heaven over one sinner who repents than over ninety-nine righteous persons' (Luke 15:7). When Jesus said this, was He referring only to the angels? Do we assume that God on His majestic throne is totally composed while He watches the heavenly beings go wild with joy? Does He comment almost indifferently, 'Oh good, there's another one in the kingdom'? Surely not!

I can imagine God leading the whole show. I can hear Him exclaiming, 'Look, angels! That guy over there is opening up his life to me. We've saved him from the jaws of hell. He's my son. Isn't that terrific?'

We have the glorious privilege of sharing Jesus with others. Many may initially reject Him, but some will respond. When that happens God wants us to know that He has used us to bring Him joy and honour. He tests your motives. If your goal is His honour your heart is pure and you are approved by God.

▓ To pray

Can you think of anyone who has fallen into the trap of living to please people?

Pause to pray for them.

Ask God to open their hearts to the truth and to help them seek His honour alone.

➤ In your notebook write down six characters or groups of people in the Bible who, at some time, were selfishly motivated and state the circumstances (e.g. James and John when they wanted to rain down fire from heaven).

➤ In your notebook write down six characters or groups of people in the Bible who, at some time, were motivated for God and state the circumstances (e.g. Barnabas when he sold a field and gave the money to the church).

The effective personal evangelist is motivated by love and loyalty to the Lord who came 'to seek and to save those who were lost'. He is moved by the fact that those without Christ are under the judgment of God. He is gripped by the fact that he has been entrusted with a message that can change their destiny from hell to heaven, and bring untold blessing into their lives and homes.
J. Oswald Sanders

It's easy — or is it?

'Get wisdom, get understanding ... Though it cost all you have, get understanding' (Prov. 4:5a,7b).

I an becomes a Christian and suddenly he's so fired up about reaching the lost that he must have a book about it.

He goes to the Christian bookshop and buys something called *Winning the Lost Made Ridiculously Easy*. (How keen we are to make things easy! One of the curses of Christianity.)

Ian studies the book and in a mechanical way tries to reproduce the techniques inside.

This particular book outlines procedures which are accompanied by illustrations. The central figure is a young man sitting alone on a park bench. He is approached by a zealous believer and the conversation goes like this:

Picture 1.
Christian: Hi! I bet you're feeling lonely.
Young man: Yes, I am.
Picture 2.
Christian: Do you ever think about spiritual things?
Young man: Oh yes. I'd like to know about God. Would you tell me?
Picture 3.
Christian: You're probably feeling that your life is very empty.

▓ To recall

What does Jesus say to suggest that the Christian life is far from easy? Give three examples (e.g. He tells us that we will be persecuted).

_____

_____

_____

▓ To meditate on

God wants you to rely, not on your knowledge, but on His Spirit.
'"Not by might nor by power, but by my Spirit," says the Lord Almighty' (Zech. 4:6).
'My message and my preaching were not with wise and persuasive words, but with a demonstration of the Spirit's power, so that your faith might not rest on men's wisdom, but on God's power' (1 Cor. 2:4,5).

Young man: Yes, I'm ready for something different.

Then the believer goes through several steps and leads the young man to Christ.

Being the keen new convert that he is, Ian decides to try it out. He goes to the park, sees a guy on a bench and goes up to him.

Ian: Hi! I bet you're feeling a bit lonely.

Young man: Not at all. I'm feeling great. Beautiful day, isn't it?

Ian: Do you ever think about spiritual things?

Young man: No. I couldn't care less.

Ian: You're probably feeling that your life is very empty.

Young man: No. I've never been doing better.

And Ian walks away wondering what's happened!

Is it wrong to have specific training principles? No. But it is wrong to rely upon them for success. If you depend on your intellectual knowledge and techniques you will fail and the devil will be laughing in your face. You don't need slick answers but the anointing of God and a deepening sensitivity to the leading of His Holy Spirit.

▓ To consider

How can a Christian cultivate a deepening sensitivity to the leading of the Holy Spirit?

_____

_____

_____

➤ If someone said to you, 'I'm interested in becoming a Christian' what Scriptures would you use to lead him to the Lord?

➤ Write them down, learn them by heart and make sure that you know where to find them.

_____

_____

_____

_____

_____

_____

... learning to lead people to faith in Christ is not merely a matter of mastering methods and techniques. There is no such thing as 'Ten Easy Lessons in Soul-Winning'. That can be a mere intellectual exercise with no personal involvement.
J. Oswald Sanders

Pray

Devote yourselves to prayer, being watchful and thankful (Col. 4:2).

(Love) ... is not easily angered, it keeps no record of wrongs ... It always protects, always trusts, always hopes, always perseveres (1 Cor. 13:5,7).

O ver the next few days I want to give you several practical insights on how to share your faith. They are based on Colossians 4:2–6.

All evangelism has its source in the realm of prayer. We hear that two and a half billion people have never even heard of Jesus, but this figure tends to remain just another statistic until we begin to pray.

As we ask God to help us experience His feelings for the unsaved He breaks in and fills us with His compassion. We are moved by the terrible needs of those around us and are motivated by love to reach them.

At the age of nineteen Paul Yonggi Cho was diagnosed as having incurable tuberculosis and given up to four months to live. A girl from high school began to visit and share Jesus with him. After several of these encounters, Paul roughly rebuked her. But she didn't run or retaliate. She simply knelt and began to weep and pray for him.

He said that when he saw her tears, his heart was deeply touched. There was clearly something different in that young girl. She was not reciting religious stories to him; she was living what she believed. Through her love and

▓ To pray

Make a list of the people whom you want to become Christians.

Pray for each of them now.

Put the list in a prominent place.

Make it your goal to continue praying regularly for them.

▓ To meditate on

God calls you to a life of prayer.
'When you pray, go into your room, close the door and pray to your Father, who is unseen. Then your Father, who sees what is done in secret, will reward you' (Matt. 6:6).
'Pray in the Spirit on all occasions with all kinds of prayers and requests. With this in mind, be alert and always keep on praying for all the saints' (Eph. 6:18).

tears he could feel the presence of God. Shortly after this he came to Christ and he now leads one of the largest churches in the world.

When I became a Christian I tried to tell my Dad about Jesus. He reacted against me, but I prayed. I commanded the devil to release him from deceiving spirits and asked God to open his heart. I began to love him and show him that I was different by the way I lived.

Then one day he opened up and I had the privilege of leading him to Christ. He was won not by words but by prayer and practical love.

God 'wants all men to be saved and to come to a knowledge of the truth' (1 Tim. 2:4). He calls you to 'stand in the gap' and pray. Cry out to Him for the salvation of your family and friends.

Call down the powers of heaven against any evil influences that surround them. 'Ask the Lord of the harvest ... to send out workers into his harvest field' (Matt. 9:38) to reach those for whom you're praying.

Discover for yourself how God engineers circumstances and blesses people in response to prayer.

➤ Read Ephesians chapter 5 and Colossians chapter 3.

➤ Using a notebook draw a line down the middle of a page. On the left-hand side, write down the things that we must reject. On the right-hand side, write down the things we must now do.

➤ If God is challenging you about anything, sort it out with Him.

▓ To do

Is your lifestyle a powerful testimony to unbelievers around you?

If not, repent of any unhelpful attitudes or actions.

Begin to express practical love to unsaved members of your family and friends.

It is doubtful if any person is saved apart from the prevailing prayer of some concerned believer.
J. Oswald Sanders

❏ STUDY 12

Personal testimony

Pray that I may proclaim it clearly, as I should (Col. 4:4).

The first thing Andrew did was to find his brother Simon and tell him, 'We have found the Messiah' (that is, the Christ). And he brought him to Jesus (John 1:41,42a).

We overcome Satan 'by the blood of the Lamb and by the word of [our] testimony' (Rev. 12:11). In other words, we understand the basic gospel message and communicate it along with personal experience.

You can share Christ without referring to yourself, but if you share from experience you will have the edge on someone who simply argues from Scripture. Paul gave his testimony three times in the book of Acts. You might not have all the theological answers but who can refute you when you say, 'My life was a mess and now I'm a new person?'

A good testimony tells someone: where you were, what happened and where you are now. It will come across with greater impact if you work on it beforehand. So divide a sheet of paper into three sections. Under 'Where I was' write down some of the more significant aspects of your life (good works, drugs, confusion, etc.) before you were saved. Under 'What happened' recall some of the key thoughts and events that led to your decision to become a Christian. Under 'Where I am now' list a few of the most important things that Jesus has done in your life since you came to know Him. Now practise

❋ To analyse

Read Acts 26:4–23.

Write down a brief outline of the different stages in Paul's testimony.

_____

_____

_____

_____

❋ To meditate on

God wants you to share with others. 'Jesus ... said, "Go home to your family and tell them how much the Lord has done for you, and how he has had mercy on you." So the man went away and began to tell ... how much Jesus had done for him' (Mark 5:19,20).
'Then ... the woman went back to the town and said to the people, "Come, see a man who told me everything I ever did"' (John 4:28,29).

it with a friend until you can present it naturally and clearly in about three minutes.

At all costs avoid jargon (saved, regeneration, reconciliation, redemption, sonship, washed in the blood ...). Your goal is not to impress your hearer but to win him. So speak simply and rely totally on the Spirit to do the impressing.

Your testimony should sound something like this: 'For twenty years I was involved in a religious institution. But on the inside I was empty and thought religion was irrelevant. One day I was hitch-hiking and a man picked me up and told me about Jesus Christ. Later, I realised I wasn't right with God and I abandoned my selfishness and surrendered myself to Him. I haven't been the same since. Jesus has revolutionised my life. He's given me ...'

When I share my testimony I try to relate to my hearer. If I speak to a young person I focus on the partying scene. If I talk to a business-man I concentrate on my pursuit of a career. If I meet a religious type I highlight my Catholic upbringing. Paul said, 'I have become all things to all men so that by all possible means I might save some' (1 Cor. 9:22).

▓ To consider

How would you angle your testimony if you were talking to:

- a young person? _____

- a businessman? _____

- a religious person? _____

> ➤ Spend time thinking about your personal testimony. Plan it as suggested above.

> ➤ Write it out in a notebook and practise it with a Christian friend.

> ➤ Pray for an opportunity to share it with a non-Christian friend. When that opportunity comes, take it.

Why is the issue of *why* being emphasised so much? Because that is what people are really interested in knowing. They do not necessarily want to know *how* you became a Christian ... the important thing most people want to know is why you placed your faith in Him and what He has done for you. In essence, they want to know how He has affected the quality of your life.
Billie Hanks Jr.

Personal tracts

... speaking the truth in love (Eph. 4:15).

(Love) is not rude (1 Cor. 13:5a).

S ome Christians are unsure about the value of tracts — and for good reason. A number of them are hideously inappropriate — particularly with regard to their title which is the first thing the unbeliever reads.

Let me give you some illustrations:

Offensive: *Go to Hell!; Hypocrite!; You're a Sinner!; What do you miss by being a Christian?* (Inside, it says *Hell.*)

Irrelevant: *What the Bible teaches about Infant Baptism.* (Inside, the pages are blank.)

Spiritual: *How I got Saved. True Religion. Blessed Assurance. Drink is a Demon.*

Bland: *Why I go to Kings Road Church. My Wonderful Experience.*

These tracts do nothing to draw people to God. If anything, they make the gospel seem irrelevant and brand Christians as foolish. In no way am I suggesting that we start handing out this sort of tract. I'm saying that we should abandon them and start designing our own.

I did that a few years ago. On the front of my personal tract are written the words, 'A moment ago we met. Was it a coincidence?' On the cover

▓ To consider

Why do you think people hand out the sort of unhelpful tracts mentioned above?

_____

_____

Do you have any literature that would offend Jesus? If so, take the appropriate action.

▓ To meditate on

God is giving you the opportunity to testify about Him on paper.

'This is the disciple who testifies to these things and who wrote them down' (John 21:24).

'In my former book, Theophilus, I wrote about all that Jesus began to do and to teach' (Acts 1:1).

'The Teacher searched to find just the right words, and what he wrote was upright and true' (Eccl. 12:10).

there's a friendly photo of me and on the back, another one of me with my family.

Sometimes I'll use the tract when there isn't really time to give my testimony. Often it backs up what I've already been sharing. Then I'll say something like, 'It's been great talking to you. When you've got a break, perhaps you'd like to read this. It's my story.'

As I walk away I'll pray, 'Father, please reveal yourself to him.'

But do tracts work? Yes, they do. An elder in a church in America became a Christian because someone gave him a personal tract. He was high on drugs at the time. But when he'd come down to earth he read the tract and immediately gave his life to Jesus.

My brother-in-law came to Christ through a tract and so too have countless other people that I know.

What an impact there would be if every believer took this idea seriously! If we all handed out only a few tracts a week, thousands would be reached in the course of a year. In eternity, wouldn't you love to hear people say, 'Thank you. Your personal tract was instrumental in bringing me to Jesus'?

➢ Using a notebook draw a line down the centre of a page. On the left-hand side, write down the vital facts that someone needs to know in order to become a Christian (e.g. God loves you). On the right-hand side, write down relevant Scriptures for each of these points.

➢ Then talk through your opinions with a Christian friend, and make any adjustments (additions or deletions) which might be necessary.

▓ To pray

If you don't already have a personal tract, pray that God will help you to write it.

If you do have one, pray each day for opportunities to use it.

The potential for blessing of a good tract should never be under-estimated.
J. Oswald Sanders

❏ STUDY 14

Writing a personal tract

And we pray this in order that you may ... please him in every way: bearing fruit in every good work, growing in the knowledge of God, being strengthened with all power according to his glorious might so that you may have great endurance and patience, and joyfully giving thanks to the Father (Col. 1:10–12).

My personal tract takes about three minutes to read and at the end it explains how you become a Christian. Some people prefer to use tracts which focus solely on their story and, as appropriate, hand out a good ready-printed gospel explanation alongside it. These personal tracts are about 450 words long and measure 14.5 cm by 10.5 cm (A6) before they're folded.

A good written testimony is not dashed off in an hour. It's the product of prayer and hard work. You may find that you have to rewrite it several times before you're happy. So don't rush it to the printer and regret it later.

Build your testimony around the three main points mentioned in study 12 and fiercely guard against all jargon and academic-sounding English. The simpler it is, the more people you will reach.

Shorter tracts will benefit from a theme, so try and focus on one aspect of your testimony (e.g. loneliness, a tragedy, a question you couldn't answer, etc.).

Your first sentence is crucial. If you start with punch you'll compel people to read on. The best way to do this is to begin by relating closely with human situations or emotions.

Example of a personal tract:

BREAKING THE MOULD
I was brought up in a comfortable middle-class home. Things were OK, but deep down I wasn't satisfied: I knew there had to be a lot more to life than just going along with the system and getting a nice job.

Rebellion. To express my rejection of my parents' values I became a punk rocker. I rebelled against society and tried to hammer out my own philosophy of life. I wanted real answers to questions about who I was and why I was here.

Confrontation. One evening in 1978, after a practice with the band I was in, I got talking to someone who told me that Jesus Christ had healed her and changed her life. I was challenged by this. I'd always assumed Jesus was dead, although I did have a vague sense that there was a God somewhere. But it was difficult to argue with someone who was evidently so happy and full of purpose.

The following week I went along to her church, expecting the service to resemble a funeral. Instead, I met genuinely warm people who really seemed to care for me — despite my bleached hair!

That evening, I heard that Jesus loved me, had died in my place, and could give me a new life. Deep down I knew this was what I was looking for.

Revolution. That night I went home and agreed with God that at heart I was a sinner, and that 'the wages of sin is death' (Rom. 6:23). Then I asked God to forgive me the wrong things I'd done and to make me a

Unless something dramatic happened at your birth, don't start your testimony there. Begin somewhere unexpected instead.

For example: *Rebellious! That was me as a teenager ...* or *The woman at the abortion clinic told me that there was nothing to worry about ...* or *I thought my honours degree would satisfy me but ...* Choose the title after you've written the tract, and remember that it's the first thing that your contact will read.

Here are a few ideas: *Brand New Start; A Quest for Reality; Is there Life after Rock 'n Roll?; Turning Point; Snatched from the Brink of Suicide; Going Nowhere; What's the Point?* Good photos or illustrations will generate interest.

At the end of the tract you could mention when and where the church meets. If you give the church office phone number make sure you have permission.

It is wiser if women do not have their address or phone number on the tract. They can write down this information at their discretion.

Before you have your tract printed show it to someone for comment. Don't be surprised if you need to alter it. An outsider may see things that you haven't noticed.

new person. Although I didn't particularly feel very different then, my life from that point began to change dramatically.

I actually found myself loving people for a change! All the aggression just seemed to disappear. God took away my foul temper and replaced it with peacefulness and real joy. My searching had come to an end. Since then, I've seen God transform many lives. And today I continue to enjoy the amazing privilege of being friends with the Creator of the Universe.

Al Shaw

Kings Church, Newtown meets at 10.30 a.m. and 7.00 p.m. on Sundays at Newtown Community Centre. For more information about the church, call Newtown 666007.

▓ Action Point

➤ Spend time preparing your personal tract.

Idea for churches
➤ Multiple testimony tracts. Ten different church members have their stories printed on one tract.

Have a good mix of people (e.g. male, female, young, old, married, single, British, ethnic, educated, disadvantaged, wealthy, poor, etc.). Have a good mix of stories (e.g. marriage break-up, healing, car accident, Christian home, anxiety, debt, involvement in a cult, convicted criminal, successful business-man, housewife, drugs, intellectual, etc.). Note: not all the stories in a tract like this need to be conversion testimonies. One or two could be about God's provision or healing.

There are four steps to accomplishment: Plan purposefully. Prepare prayerfully. Proceed positively. Pursue persistently.

Be wise

Be wise in the way you act towards outsiders (Col. 4:5a).

Take heed, you senseless ones among the people; you fools, when will you become wise? (Ps. 94:8)

W hen I became a Christian I was like a bull in a china shop and I offended a lot of people. One of the first sermons I heard was about not laying up for yourself treasure on earth. I immediately went home and told my mother that we should consider withdrawing money from our bank account to give to a church I attended. Then I got together all my sister's cigarettes, dipped them in vinegar and put them back in her room! Needless to say, they weren't exactly drawn to Jesus!

A friend and I went to a rough area of town and rounded up a few prostitutes. We told them that we'd give them money if they'd sit for ten minutes and listen to us. Then we preached the gospel at them! We had no church backing and no wisdom. We were just plain stupid!

How many of us have read stirring biographies of great men and women of God and have tried in vain to imitate their zeal and devotion? It doesn't work because we're latching onto the experience of someone else and applying it to ourselves. We're in bondage to their faith when God wants to speak to us direct. Indeed, the biography may tell us that our hero got up to pray at 4.00 a.m. but omits

▓ To consider

Have you offended anyone by the way you have witnessed in the past?
Be reconciled (e.g. see the person or send a letter of apology).

▓ To meditate on

God wants you to seek His wisdom. 'But the wisdom that comes from heaven is first of all pure; then peace-loving, considerate, submissive, full of mercy and good fruit, impartial and sincere' (James 3:17).
'If any of you lacks wisdom, he should ask God, who gives generously to all without finding fault, and it will be given to him' (James 1:5).

to mention that he went to bed at 6.00 p.m.

Jesus said, 'I will make you fishers of men' (Mark 1:17). We need wisdom and sensitivity to know when and how to fish. Sometimes God may say, 'I'm not asking you to share your faith with anybody today.' On another occasion you might be speaking to someone who starts resisting you and God says, 'You've planted a seed, now back off.'

God convicted me about the way I had hurt people. I apologised to them. When my sister was saved, we asked our parents to forgive us for being selfish, disrespectful and rebellious. As a result, many barriers crumbled and our confession paved the way for their conversion.

Are you struggling to reach your friends and relatives now because you used sledge-hammer evangelism when you were first saved? Are there unresolved conflicts with them that are unrelated to your past evangelistic activities?

Whatever the reason for the rift, God is asking you to be reconciled. Don't wait for feelings. Take the initiative and focus on the part that you have played in the situation. 'Blessed are the peacemakers, for they will be called sons of God' (Matt. 5:9).

✸ To pray

Meditate on Proverbs 3:5–8.

Are you having difficulties witnessing at work or among your friends or neighbours?

Pray now that God will give you great wisdom.

➢ Read Proverbs chapters 1–9 and hear Jesus, your wisdom (1 Cor. 1:24), speaking to you.

➢ Write down anything specific that He is saying to you.

... the Lord ... has revealed to the sons of men where true wisdom lies, and we have in it the text, 'Whoso trusteth in the Lord, happy is he' (Prov. 16:20). The true way to handle a matter wisely is to trust in the Lord. This is the sure clue to the most intricate labyrinths of life.
C. H. Spurgeon

Make friends

God is love. Whoever lives in love lives in God, and God in him ... love is made complete among us (1 John 4:16b,17a).

The commandments ... are summed up in this one rule: 'Love your neighbour as yourself' (Rom. 13:9).

P hysically Jesus wasn't a particularly attractive person. 'He had ... nothing in his appearance that we should desire him' (Isa. 53:2b). But He had something that drew the crowds. What was it? Love.

Jesus was a 'friend of ... "sinners"' (Matt. 11:19b). He accepted them as they were and took a real interest in their lives. He is our example. If we are wise, we will make friends before we make converts.

It's been discovered that 85 per cent of all genuine converts come to Christ through a friend. When 240 people were asked, 'How did you perceive the one who led you to the Lord?' 170 of them said, 'As a friend'. Converts who fail to make friends tend to backslide because they feel unloved.

Today people talk about having a 'burden for the lost'. Apparently we're supposed to feel the heavy weight of it. But what happens when the feeling has gone? No. It's not a burden on us; it's compassion within us. God pours out His love into our hearts (Rom. 5:5) and we willingly share that love with others.

Before my sister became a Christian she was a hard-hearted near-alcoholic who was very

▓ To do

Befriend an unbeliever of your own sex.

Write down how you can show love to him/her (e.g. go out for a coffee, help with a need).

_____

_____

Act on your ideas.

▓ To meditate on

Jesus wants His love to be in you and to overflow to others through you.
'I ... will continue to make you known in order that the love you have for me may be in them' (John 17:26).
'May the Lord make your love increase and overflow for each other and for everyone else' (1 Thess. 3:12).
'Greater love has no-one than this, that he lay down his life for his friends' (John 15:13).

wary of my conversion. She had every reason to be sceptical. She knew me — and my life hadn't displayed much love and self-sacrifice. How did I win her?

I invited her on holiday with me and paid for everything. When she saw my love, her heart began to soften. It wasn't long before I was able to talk about Jesus and help her to know Him.

You will earn the right to be heard if you take a genuine interest in the people you want to reach. So if you hear that someone in your neighbourhood has had a baby, don't go round clutching a tract. Offer to help. Say, 'I and a group of my friends from the church would be happy to take care of a few things for a while. Perhaps we could prepare some evening meals and do some washing ...' Evangelism like this is bound to win hearts.

When you simply try to reach out and serve people, evangelising the world suddenly sounds very simple. It is simple. It's just you befriending people, loving them and sharing Jesus with them as God gives you the opportunity. Jesus said, 'Let your light shine before men, that they may see your good deeds and praise your Father in heaven' (Matt. 5:16).

➤ Read 1 Samuel 18:1–4; 19:1–7; 20; 23:15–18; 2 Samuel 1:26.

➤ From these verses pick out the characteristics of friendship in the life of Jonathan.

▓ To encourage

Send a card to a close friend stating how much you value his/her friendship.

Write below any ways in which your friendship could be enhanced (e.g. more prayer together, greater degree of honesty).

_____

_____

Evangelism flows out of a well-balanced life. Your friendliness will allow people to identify with you in a natural way. People are attracted to those who know how to laugh, sing, engage in athletics, and enjoy just being *real*.
Billie Hanks Jr.

Divine appointments

Make the most of every opportunity (Col. 4:5b).

Always be prepared to give an answer to everyone who asks you to give the reason for the hope that you have (1 Pet. 3:15).

Divine appointments are sovereignly arranged opportunities with people to help them discover new life in Jesus Christ. Many Christians don't recognise divine appointments. They go through each day unaware that God is sovereignly arranging opportunities for them to share the gospel.

There are two main reasons why I seem to have so many divine appointments. First, I expect them. I know how much God longs to fulfil His Great Commission through me so I believe that He will guide me into conversations about Him. Whenever I'm with someone for more than a few minutes I ask myself, 'Is this a divine appointment?' Usually it is. If I don't have much time to talk, I hand the individual my personal tract and encourage him to read it.

Second, I'm ready. God knows that I'm prepared to share the gospel with anyone, anytime, anywhere. Occasionally I'll talk to a famous person. More often it will be to an ordinary individual. I've discovered that many divine appointments come as unwelcome interruptions. But I'm Christ's ambassador and, given any chance, I will speak for Him.

Sometimes people come to you and ask

▓ To consider

Where can you see possible divine appointments in your life (e.g. with someone in the supermarket checkout queue, particular colleagues at work or friends at school)?

_____

_____

_____

▓ To meditate on

God wants you to know that He has sovereignly planned things for you. 'For we are God's workmanship, created in Christ Jesus to do good works, which God prepared in advance for us to do' (Eph. 2:10). 'Let us throw off everything that hinders and the sin that so easily entangles, and let us run with perseverance the race marked out for us' (Heb. 12:1b).

what's different about you; more often you'll create the opportunities. Once I went to pay for my meal at the cash desk in a restaurant. I thanked the woman standing there for the food and added, 'I suppose you can tell I'm American. Can you guess what I'm doing in England?' I told her that I was preaching at a conference and explained that I'd had an encounter with Jesus Christ. She listened for about a minute, then tears began to well up in her eyes. As I left I prayed, 'Lord, open her heart. Give her the gift of repentance.'

Evangelism isn't a burden; it's an adventure. Nothing that happens to you is an accident. The Bible teaches that 'A man's steps are directed by the Lord' (Prov. 20:24). Every day God is supernaturally guiding you. Don't see your contacts as 'random encounters' but as divine appointments. Make the most of them.

From now on when you get up in the morning pray, 'Father, it's an honour to serve you. You've planned divine appointments for me today and I'm not going to turn my back on them. Prompt me by your Spirit. Help me to know what to say. I believe you're going to use me to spread the good news wherever I go.'

➤ With reference to evangelism, what lessons do you learn from these verses: Ps. 126:5,6; Eccl. 11:6; Hos. 10:12; John 4: 36–38; Gal. 6:9?

▓ **To resolve**

Write out and memorise Matthew 10:32.

_____

_____

_____

From today, make it your goal to pray for and expect divine appointments. Ask God to help you overcome your nervousness and reach out in faith.

Lifestyle evangelism: taking the initiative to help (not make or force) a person move one step closer to Jesus Christ.
Larry Tomczak

☐ STUDY 18

Speak with grace

Let your conversation be always full of grace, seasoned with salt (Col. 4:6a).

Moses said to the LORD, 'O Lord, I ... am slow of speech and tongue.' The LORD said to him, 'Who gave man his mouth?' (Exod. 4:10,11a)

I love to teach people to relate naturally to unbelievers. So often we walk away from divine appointments simply because we're afraid.

We think, 'He's not going to be interested in Jesus Christ. Anyway, I don't know how to start a conversation, let alone cope with it when it's under way.'

If you think that people aren't interested in Jesus Christ, you're believing a lie. Certainly people don't want religion, phoney rules and lifeless formulae, but they do want new life. Jesus longs to draw people to Himself through you. If you put flesh on Him by your lifestyle, they'll listen. If you accept them where they are and show genuine interest in them they'll be wide open. The Bible says that 'Pleasant speech increases persuasiveness' (Prov. 16:21 RSV).

Jesus was a master of communication. Early in His ministry we read that 'All spoke well of him and were amazed at the gracious words that came from his lips' (Luke 4:22). He knew how to relate to people, to speak to them.

His words were salty — they made you thirsty for more. Jesus wants your conversation to be full of grace and salt.

▓ To reflect

Recall three occasions when Jesus spoke graciously to someone.

1. _____

2. _____

3. _____

▓ To meditate on

God wants you to speak graciously. 'Words from a wise man's mouth are gracious' (Eccl. 10:12).
'A word aptly spoken is like apples of gold in settings of silver' (Prov. 25:11).
'Do not let any unwholesome talk come out of your mouths, but only what is helpful for building others up according to their needs, that it may benefit those who listen' (Eph. 4:29).

So you don't go up to someone and hit him with hellfire and judgement or launch into restoration principles and being a prophetic people. You relate to him. As appropriate, you talk about the economy, current events, holidays, the music scene ... If he has children with him, you take an interest in them. When you've expressed friendship, then you can share enough of your testimony to make him curious to know more.

Once I went up to a group of punk rockers in Trafalgar Square and began chatting with one of them. He had a Mohican hairstyle and after a while I gently asked him how he got his hair like that. I joked a bit with him and said that I used to play in a band.

Then, when I knew he felt accepted, I tossed in the salt. 'I thought I was doing OK but I've since found something better — a real peace and purpose in life. If you've got a few minutes, I'd be glad to tell you what happened to me.' Before I left I gave him my personal tract.

Pray that God will make you not so much a witness as a lover of people. When you show interest in them and speak kindly, they'll listen to what you have to say.

➤ In a notebook, divide the page into two columns. Then write down from the following verses in the Psalms:
a) what the psalmist has decided to do
b) how often he's decided to do it:
Ps. 34:1; 35:28; 44:8; 89:1,2; 145:2.

➤ Now look at Psalm 71 and write down, using the notebook, what David has decided he will say concerning God.

▓ To consider

What four things in Psalm 15:1–4 must a person do or beware of doing with his tongue if he wants to live in God's presence?

1. _____

2. _____

3. _____

4. _____

Kindness is a warm breeze in a frigid climate, a radiant heat that melts the icebergs of fear, distrust, and unhappiness.

Be able to answer everyone

... so that you may
know how to answer
everyone (Col. 4:6b).

Don't have anything to
do with foolish and
stupid arguments,
because you know
they produce quarrels
(2 Tim. 2:23).

People will have genuine objections to the
gospel message. But before we look at them,
let's consider how to react to the questioner.

Be confident. You will be surprised at how
much you already know. As you step out in
faith, God will honour you. When you're in a
tight situation His Holy Spirit will be there to
help you.

Don't argue. Some unbelievers are totally
disinterested in the gospel. You will start
talking to them about Jesus and they will
simply quarrel with you and try to make you
look foolish. Some of them may even be drunk
or high on drugs. In your attempt to answer,
you may become argumentative which, in turn,
will make you feel guilty. Jesus said, ' Do not
throw your pearls to pigs' (Matt. 7:6a). He has
not called you into heated debates with hostile
people. Unless you have a very clear word from
God, excuse yourself from the conversation but
leave them with a copy of your personal tract.

Don't worry. When someone raises an
objection for which you have no answer, the
devil will try hard to make you feel stupid.
Don't let him discourage you. Affirm the person
who raised the query by saying, 'That's a good

▓ To avoid

According to 1 Tim. 1:4; 6:4,5; Titus 3:9,
what is it not helpful to discuss?

_____

_____

According to the same verses, what do
discussions about these things
promote?

_____

▓ To meditate on

God wants you to trust Him as you
speak.
'I am the Lord your God ... Open wide
your mouth and I will fill it' (Ps. 81:10).
'Pray also for me, that whenever I open
my mouth, words may be given me so
that I will fearlessly make known the
mystery of the gospel ... Pray that I may
declare it fearlessly, as I should' (Eph.
6:19,20).

question. I'm sure that there's an answer but I
don't know what it is so I'll try and find out for
you. If we could meet again on Thursday ...'
Your honesty will probably accomplish more
than eloquent guesswork.

Be respectful. Treat your questioner with
respect. Be genuinely interested in him. 'For
with the measure you use, it will be measured
to you' (Luke 6:38b).

Walk in the Spirit. Remember that the
battle is not merely intellectual; it is spiritual
(Eph. 6:12). You are trying to snatch people
from the jaws of hell and Satan will do all he
can to oppose you. He blinds the minds of
unbelievers (2 Cor. 4:4), so pray as you speak
to them. If you sense a demonic spirit, release
the power of God against it. Say in your heart,
'In the name of Jesus I take authority over any
hindering spirit.' This can have quite a
dramatic effect on people's understanding —
not always immediately, but often eventually.

Do not just read about the objections people
raise but get together with a Christian friend
and role-play each one. Then, when you face
the objection for real, you will be more likely to
remember what to say.

➤ Write down what
you learn from the
following verses which
have in common the
theme of 'answering':
Prov. 15:28; 16:1; 18:13;
26:4; Eccl. 3:7; Matt.
22:46; 27:12–14;
Luke 2:47; 20:26; 23:9;
1 Pet. 3:15.

▓ To consider

Recall three occasions when three different Bible
characters gave wise answers to their questioners.

1. person: _____

    occasion: _____

2. person: _____

    occasion: _____

3. person: _____

    occasion: _____

I cannot argue while men
die. I do not know who the
man on the 'Jericho Road'
is. I do not know who hit
him nor where or why. I
only know, there he is! He
may not be a member of
our tribe, our group, our
convention, but he needs
my help, and I must help
him!
Oscar Johnson

'What about the heathen?'

Indeed, when Gentiles, who do not have the law, do by nature things required by the law, they are a law for themselves, even though they do not have the law, since they show that the requirements of the law are written on their hearts, their consciences also bearing witness, and their thoughts now accusing, now even defending them (Rom. 2:14,15).

The question *What about those who haven't heard?* is usually a smoke-screen. The Spirit is beginning to bring conviction to your questioner. He feels uncomfortable and tries to turn the spotlight away from himself and onto someone else in the world. The woman of Samaria did a similar thing. When Jesus challenged her about her private life she changed the subject (John 4:18–20).

Before you answer the question, affirm it. Say something encouraging like, 'That's a good question. I used to wonder the same thing.' Then move on as quickly as you can.

Tell him that God is just and fair. 'The judgments of the LORD are true; they are righteous altogether' (Ps. 19:9b NASB). Then point out from Romans 2:14,15 that everyone in the world is given some understanding of right and wrong. We know when we have sinned because our consciences make us feel guilty. Explain also that God 'rewards those who earnestly seek him' (Heb. 11:6).

Now look briefly at the sincere man who has never heard of Jesus. There he is in a remote part of the world. He instinctively feels that he has done wrong and is sorry. He tries to obey

▓ To consider

Sometimes we are puzzled that God allows so much injustice to go on around us. Consider God's absolute justice reflected in: Deut. 32:4; Ps. 89:14; Isa. 9:7 and John 5:30.

If you are experiencing injustice, commit your cause to God in faith. If you are behaving unjustly towards someone else, do something about it.

▓ To meditate on

God wants you to consider Him. 'Will not the Judge of all the earth do right?' (Gen. 18:25) 'You will seek me and find me when you seek me with all your heart' (Jer. 29:13). 'There is a judge for the one who rejects me and does not accept my words; that very word which I spoke will condemn him at the last day' (John 12:48).

the moral law that is written in his heart and diligently cries out to the Creator God for help.

Cornelius 'and all his family were devout and God-fearing' (Acts 10:2). Just as God sent Peter to Cornelius, so He can make Himself known to the searching individual in an obscure region. What happens? A tract or portion of Scripture may fall into the man's hands, or someone may go to his village to tell his people about Jesus.

God has given evidence of Himself through creation (Rom. 1:20), and through our conscience (Rom. 2:15). All men fail to respond to God as they should, and that is why all men need Christ. If they have not heard the Word, there is indication that their conscience and their response to it will be taken into account by an all-just God (Rom. 2:15).

Now bring the focus of attention back to your questioner. Remind him that God is just and that He will judge everyone according to the light that he has received.

Say something like this, 'God wants everyone to hear about Jesus, but right now He's giving you some understanding. Your concern is not what will happen to those who haven't heard but what you will do with what you've heard.'

▨ To reflect

Is God trying to draw your attention to something but you keep changing the subject (e.g. tithing, a relationship, your prayer life, etc.)?

Face the issue squarely and do something about it.

... the Bible gives no detailed answer to this question for a very good reason. If a person has a Bible in the first place, or has access to a Bible, then he has heard or he can find out; and the Bible is absolutely clear about his position. The discussion of the destiny of those who have never heard, by those who have heard, is academic. Each of us has to give an account of his own life according to his own opportunities.
David Watson

'I don't believe in God'

The heavens declare the glory of God; the skies proclaim the work of his hands (Ps. 19:1).

Some people don't want to believe God exists because they know that they will be held accountable to Him for their actions. Their problem is not so much intellectual as moral.

Point to a manufactured object — a building or a car, maybe. Suggest to the atheist that there has to be a designer or an inventor behind them. Then ask gently if it is logical to believe that the world was just thrown together haphazardly. Can there possibly be a creation without a Creator?

God reveals Himself through the universe and through the Scriptures.

Look at Psalm 19 and encourage the atheist to consider the complexity, harmony and order of the universe. Who fixes the laws? How is it possible to predict the exact time of the sunrise? How can anyone see the birth of a baby and say, 'There is no God'?

The Psalm directs our attention to the sun. An emperor once said to a Jewish Rabbi, 'If there's a God, I want to see him.' The Rabbi took him outside at midday and told him to look at the sun. 'I can't do that,' said the emperor. 'The light will blind me.'

The Rabbi replied, 'If you can't look at one of

▧ To appreciate

Begin to cultivate a deeper awareness of God's glory in creation.

• Look more closely at beautiful things.
• Listen to the birds.
• Smell the fragrance of a rose.
• Touch the intricate petals of a flower.
• Enjoy the flavour of good food.

Read Psalm 104.

▧ To meditate on

God wants you to consider Him.
'For since the creation of the world God's invisible qualities — his eternal power and divine nature — have been clearly seen, being understood from what has been made, so that men are without excuse' (Rom. 1:20).
'O LORD, our LORD, how majestic is your name in all the earth! You have set your glory above the heavens' (Ps. 8:1).

God's messengers, how can you possibly look on the glory of God Himself?'

You may say to your questioner, 'If you're struggling to see God in the physical world, you can know Him in the Bible. Two thousand years ago He became a man — I'd be happy to tell you about Him.' If, after that, he still insists that he is an atheist, share the 'circle of knowledge' illustration.

Draw a large circle on a piece of paper and label it 'All the knowledge in the universe'.

Ask him to draw a circle inside the large one to reflect how much of this knowledge he personally knows.

Then say, 'Isn't it possible that in that wide expanse outside your personal knowledge there just might be a God?' If he concedes this, he is not an atheist but an agnostic — someone who isn't sure. If you can bring him this far, he may be more receptive to the rest of your gospel presentation.

He may allow you to pray for him — that God will reveal Himself. But if he rejects the gospel, pray for him later.

Ask God to pull down the strongholds, open his heart and grant him the gift of repentance.

➤ Role-play.

➤ Memorise Scripture.

▓ To consider

Review the pace of your life.

Do you take time to relax or meditate on God? Are you too preoccupied with anything (e.g. television, sports activities, cinema-going, etc.)?

Ask God to reveal to you how He wants you to organise your time (e.g. a new hobby, more exercise, Bible study one evening a week, hospitality two Sundays out of four, etc.).

The existence of a watch argues the existence of a watchmaker. The sound of harmonious music argues for the existence of a musician. The existence of a harmoniously running universe, vast in magnitude yet perfect in detail, argues the existence of an infinitely wise and powerful Creator-God — for every effect must have an adequate cause.
J. Oswald Sanders

'I don't believe the Bible'

'What must I do to
inherit eternal life?'
(Luke 10:25b)

S ociety declares, 'There are no absolutes.
Man decides what is right and wrong.' We
say, 'There are absolutes. God gives us His
standards in the Bible.'

Often a person who disputes the authenticity
of the Scriptures is suffering from intellectual
pride. Tell him that he has a right to his views
but point out that the Bible is one of the most
highly valued literary works. If he is saying that
it isn't reliable, then he should be questioning
the works of Aristotle, Plato and Socrates.

Say to him, 'You may not believe the Bible,
but its central message is to tell people how
they can have eternal life. Do you know what it
teaches about that?' He may reply, 'I don't
believe in eternal life.' You then say, 'That
wasn't my question. I'm just asking if you know
what this book teaches about it. An intelligent
person is not going to reject something without
at least understanding what it's saying.'

He will probably suggest: 'Keeping the Ten
Commandments, imitating Christ, following
moral teaching like the Beatitudes and loving
your neighbour.' You can then graciously
correct his error and say, 'According to the
Scriptures, that's not how you can have eternal

▓ To consider

What Scriptures would you share with
someone on the subject of eternal life?
(Don't write down more than six
references.)
John 3:16; _____

_____

_____

▓ To meditate on

God wants you to be sure of His Word.
'All Scripture is God-breathed and is
useful for teaching, rebuking,
correcting and training in
righteousness' (2 Tim. 3:16).
'The word of God is living and active.
Sharper than any double-edged sword,
it penetrates even to dividing soul and
spirit, joints and marrow; it judges the
thoughts and attitudes of the heart'
(Heb. 4:12).

life. Surely you wouldn't reject a book until you knew what it said?'

Someone who claims that the Bible is full of contradictions needs to be asked if he has read it. If he has, and can point out some of the inconsistencies, offer to look at them. 'Were there two demon-possessed men or just one?' (Matt. 8:28; Luke 8:27) This may not be a contradiction. To one friend I may say, 'Yesterday I saw the mayor and chief of police' and to another I may say, 'Yesterday I saw the mayor.' If these two friends meet and exchange stories, they might accuse me of lying. A difference in perspective cannot always be labelled, 'a contradiction'. Four witnesses to an event will each give a different account.

If your questioner comments, 'The Bible is too hard to understand and you can't take it literally,' say, 'If you mean some of the strange symbolism, I agree. But you only take the Bible literally where you're supposed to. Jesus is not actually "the door". He's giving a picture of Himself. But let's look at John 3:16. How many mysterious interpretations are there of that?'

Now you can explain the message of salvation.

▓ To challenge

There are many ways to encounter God through His word, e.g. hearing, singing, preaching, reading, studying, meditating, memorising.

In what area(s) do you sense that God is challenging you?

What action are you going to take?

Voltaire tried to crush Christianity. He said that in one hundred years there would not be a Bible on the face of the earth. A century later, Voltaire was gone and the American Bible Society had set up their Geneva head-quarters on the site of his former home.
Larry Tomczak

'Jesus: the only way to God?'

'But small is the gate and narrow the road that leads to life, and only a few find it' (Matt. 7:14).

'Salvation is found in no-one else, for there is no other name under heaven given to men by which we must be saved' (Acts 4:12).

For it is by grace you have been saved, through faith— and this not from yourselves, it is the gift of God — not by works, so that no-one can boast (Eph. 2:8,9).

When Christians claim that Jesus is the only way to God, they are often accused of being bigoted and narrow. An unbeliever cannot accept that devout Buddhists, Hindus and Muslims will be lost unless they come to Jesus.

Tell your questioner, 'I know it sounds narrow but truth is narrow.' Two plus two equals four. You can't say, 'Let's be open-minded about this and make the answer seventeen.' To produce water you need two elements of hydrogen and one of oxygen. You can't say, 'We'll have five of hydrogen and twenty-three of oxygen.' You won't get what you want.

Explain that you'd love to be able to tell him that everyone gets to God in the end, but that this is not true. Jesus said, 'I am the way and the truth and the life. No-one comes to the Father except through me' (John 14:6). You are not being bigoted, you are being faithful to the truth.

When a pilot flies into an airport he doesn't suddenly decide to land in the park. He lines up with a narrow runway. In the same way we don't choose what we believe, we line up with the truth.

✸ To consider

In what areas are we exhorted to be sincere? (Four one-word answers).

Rom. 12:9 _____

Eph. 6:5 _____

1 Tim. 1:5 _____

Heb. 10:22 _____

Are you sincere in these areas?

✸ To meditate on

God wants you to know the truth about sin.
'For the wages of sin is death, but the gift of God is eternal life in Christ Jesus our Lord' (Rom. 6:23).
'If you do not believe that (I am the one I claim to be), you will indeed die in your sins' (John 8:24).
'Make every effort to enter through the narrow door, because many, I tell you, will try to enter and will not be able to' (Luke 13:24).

Your questioner may still insist, 'All religions are the same.' But they are not. Other religions do not acknowledge the deity of Jesus Christ and the free gift of salvation.

'Jesus is a god,' they say. 'You earn your way to heaven.' But the Bible teaches that Jesus is God incarnate and that salvation is by grace — God's **R**iches **A**t **C**hrist's **E**xpense.

'I think sincerity is what really matters,' says your questioner. Well, Hitler was sincere and look at the devastation he caused. Sincere people have taken prescribed drugs to help them and have gone through terrible suffering as a result. You can sincerely believe that you can drive over a level crossing before the train comes — and kill your family in the process. People can be sincerely wrong.

The Word tells us, 'There is a way that seems right to a man, but in the end it leads to death' (Prov. 16:25). However pious a person may seem, he is lost without Christ.

Try to help your questioner to see that you're not being intolerant of others.

Jesus is the only way to God. That's the truth. No compromise!

➤ Role-play.

➤ Memorise Scripture.

▓ To pray

Spend some time praying for God to give revelation of the truth to people who belong to:

• alternative religions
• cults.

Ask God to help those whose sons or daughters are wrapped up in cult movements. If you know any parents personally, write to them sharing your concern and, if appropriate, assuring them of your prayer support.

... there is no plan of deliverance except by Jesus Christ, the Saviour of sinners. In vain you climb to the highest pinnacles of your self-conceit and your worldly merit: you shall be drowned — for 'other foundation can no man lay than that which is laid — Jesus Christ and Him crucified.'
C. H. Spurgeon

'Why does evil exist?'

'He has anointed me to preach good news to the poor' (Luke 4:18a).

You want something but don't get it. You kill and covet, but you cannot have what you want (James 4:2).

The questioner points to poverty, war and sickness and blames God for it. He reasons, 'If He is good, He should stop it; if He is almighty, He would prevent it in the first place.'

You may have to admit that you don't understand why God allows some dreadful things to happen. But the root cause of the world's problems has to do not with God, but with man. God's creation was 'very good'. There was no sin, sickness or tragedy. God wanted man to serve Him, but man rebelled and went his own way. Succeeding generations have become proud, selfish and greedy.

The plight of the hungry in India would be greatly relieved if they killed and ate their cows. But their religion forbids this. The famine-torn nation of Ethiopia would not be hungry if governments pulled together to help them. There would be sufficient resources for everyone if the rich lived more simply, sold their luxuries and gave the money to the poor. Poverty is a curse. We cannot blame God for it.

When we hear of wars and riots, we are wrong to declare, 'It's God's fault.' James says that fights and quarrels come from the desires which battle within us. We are greedy for power

▓ To consider

Do you doubt God's goodness? Bring to mind all the good things He gives you and does for you.

Read Ephesians 5:20 and Philippians 4:4.

Cultivate a spirit of praise and gratitude regardless of what happens to you.

▓ To meditate on

God wants you to know His grace. 'The wrath of God is being revealed from heaven against all the godlessness and wickedness of men who suppress the truth by their wickedness' (Rom. 1:18).
'You are a gracious and compassionate God, slow to anger and abounding in love, a God who relents from sending calamity' (Jonah 4:2b).

or money. In America there was a widespread blackout one night and the people went wild. They robbed, fought and killed each other. Why? Because man's nature is selfish. Unbelievers need laws to restrain them. But if everyone in the world became a Christian and lived like Jesus, there would be no war or violence.

God is not behind abortion either. He hates the shedding of innocent blood. Someone says, 'Maybe the Bible is against sex outside marriage. I don't care. I'm going to have a good time.' Then one day his girlfriend tells him she's pregnant. 'That's inconvenient,' he thinks. 'Never mind, we'll just abort it.' This is nothing to do with God.

The woman now sitting paralysed in a wheelchair was completely healthy until she was run over by a drunk. The family was happy until mummy went off with another man. Little Emily was doing well at school until her father began to abuse her. God is love and these things break His heart. He could have created us like robots who were programmed to obey Him. But He wanted a relationship with people who loved Him by choice.

▓ To do

Ask God to stir compassion in the hearts of born-again government officials and pray that we, as His church, be sensitive to the Spirit's leadings to make generous financial contributions to help relieve suffering, poverty and human need in our world.

Out of your concern, pray for labourers to go out into the harvest.

Consider your own practical response.

Christ conceived the human soul to be of such transcendent value that He willingly exchanged the glories of heaven for a life of poverty, suffering, shame and death, rather than that one person should perish. In one scale He placed the world and all it could offer of fame and riches and pleasure, and in the other a human life, and He declared the scale went down on the side of the soul.
J. Oswald Sanders

❏ STUDY 25

'Father Abraham, have pity on me and send Lazarus to dip the tip of his finger in water and cool my tongue, because I am in agony in this fire' (Luke 16:24).

'But hell doesn't exist!'

Psychologists say that we tend to deny the things that we fear the most. Some people refuse to go to the doctor because they are afraid of what he might find. The first reaction of a bereaved person is denial — 'It hasn't happened. I can't believe it.'

When you are confronted with the subject of hell, be honest. Say that you are not there to preach hellfire and brimstone, but make it clear that there is a hell. Jesus spoke about it more than heaven.

Your questioner may say, 'Well, I don't think you'd be conscious in hell.' Then point out from Luke 16:19–31 that the rich man in hell was very conscious! He didn't experience some vague existence. It was torment. Jesus tells us that hell is the place where the 'fire never goes out' (Mark 9:43).

You may be asked, 'Why does God send people to hell?' Then explain that hell was never intended for man. It was 'prepared for the devil and his angels' (Matt. 25:41).

God does not carelessly condemn people to hell. They send themselves there when they shun His provision in Jesus Christ and His free gift of eternal life. Hell is the greatest

▦ To pray

Pray about the following evils in your nation:

- demonic activity (covens, occult practices, etc.)
- sexual immorality
- homosexuality
- abortion
- child abuse
- drug and alcohol abuse
- any other evil practices that come to mind.

▦ To meditate on

God wants you to recognise the reality of hell.
'Do not be afraid of those who kill the body but cannot kill the soul. Rather, be afraid of the One who can destroy both soul and body in hell' (Matt. 10:28).
'If anyone's name was not found written in the book of life, he was thrown into the lake of fire' (Rev. 20:15).

Action point

➤ Role-play.

➤ Memorise Scripture.

monument to free will that there is. Through it God says, 'I love you, but I'm willing to release you to go your own way if you don't want to follow me.'

You might use an illustration like this: 'I could train my children like puppets and force them to obey me. I could tell them, "Right, every night you must kiss me before you go to bed." I would get the kisses but they would be cold and impersonal, and the exercise would bring none of us any pleasure.

'But if I gave them the freedom to choose, they would voluntarily throw themselves into my arms and love me.'

Continue: 'God could demand to be obeyed. But this is not love. Love is voluntarily given. Jesus voluntarily gave His life for you. You and I deserved to be punished for our sins, but Jesus died on the cross as our substitute. Deep inside you know that you're living apart from God. He made you a free agent and will let you go to hell if you want to.

'But since He loves you, He will do all He can to draw you to Himself. If you surrender your will to Him He will forgive you and revolutionise your life.'

To consider

Look up Psalm 23 — if possible, a modern translation which you don't normally use.

Read the Psalm and meditate on the words.

Let God speak to you.

The safest road to hell is the gradual one — the gentle slope, soft underfoot, without sudden turnings, without milestones, without signposts.
C. S. Lewis

'Jesus rose from the dead?'

If you confess with your mouth, 'Jesus is Lord,' and believe in your heart that God raised him from the dead, you will be saved (Rom. 10:9).

'You are to say, "His disciples came during the night and stole him away while we were asleep"' (Matt. 28:13).

The resurrection is the cornerstone of our faith. The person who questions it needs to be reminded that it was a historical fact that did not take place in a corner. Over five hundred people saw the resurrected Christ at the same time. Here are some of the theories of what happened and arguments to refute them:

The disciples stole the body. People might die for the truth but rarely for a lie. If the disciples had stolen the body they would not have been willing to suffer for a story that they knew to be false. At the least sign of persecution they would have said, 'We tried to fool you. Actually we stole Jesus' body. It's over here.' But all of the disciples were prepared to die for truth — and most of them did.

The authorities stole the body. When the authorities saw people believing in Jesus they were very angry. If they had stolen the body they could have halted the rumour about the resurrection simply by parading it through the streets. The fact is they had no body to produce.

The disciples hallucinated. Usually people hallucinate about things that they want to take place. A mother who loses her son might

▓ **To consider**

Read 1 Corinthians 15:12–58.

If you are struggling with the subject of death, ask God to help you.

If necessary, talk through your feelings with someone.

▓ **To meditate on**

God wants you to be sure.
'Jesus said ... "I am the resurrection and the life. He who believes in me will live, even though he dies; and whoever lives and believes in me will never die"' (John 11:25,26).
'Christ died for our sins ... he was buried ... he was raised on the third day according to the Scriptures' (1 Cor. 15:3b,4).

hallucinate and 'see him'. She projects unreality. But after the crucifixion the disciples went back to their jobs. They accepted that Jesus was dead. Indeed, Thomas actually refused to believe that He was alive.

Jesus never died. The Romans were masters at crucifixion. They had crucified enough people to know when their victim was dead. In any case, Jesus could not possibly have revived after the treatment He received. He went through an excruciating death. The Bible says that 'his appearance was ... disfigured beyond that of any man and his form marred beyond human likeness' (Isa. 52:14). He would not have had the strength to remove the stone from the entrance of the tomb and overcome the guards.

Today millions of Christians claim, 'I know Jesus rose from the dead.' They can say this not simply because they have read it in the Bible but because He has forgiven their sins and adopted them as His sons.

Tell your questioner that your life has been transformed not by an empty theory or philosophy but by the power of the risen Christ. He can't refute your personal testimony.

▧ To pray

Pray for and, if appropriate, visit those you know who, through age or sickness, are coming to the end of their lives.

- If they are not Christians, pray that God will give them revelation of Himself.
- If they are Christians, pray that they will see death not as tragic loss, but as glorious gain (Phil. 1:21).

Pray too that God will comfort the relatives of anyone who has recently died. Send a card expressing your love and, if appropriate, your prayer support.

> Role-play.

> Memorise Scripture.

In Glendale, California, at Forest Lawn Cemetery hundreds of people each year stand before two huge paintings. One pictures the crucifixion of Christ. The other depicts His resurrection. In the second painting the artist has pictured an empty tomb with an angel near the entrance. In the foreground stands the figure of the risen Christ. But the striking feature of that huge canvas is a vast throng of people, back in the misty background, stretching into the distance and out of sight, suggesting the multitude who will be raised from the dead because Jesus first died and rose for them.
George Sweeting

'Is Jesus God?'

In the beginning was the Word, and the Word was with God, and the Word was God (John 1:1).

People who belong to other religions and cults may esteem Jesus but they certainly do not see Him as equal with God. You might point to John 1:1 and say, 'Jesus is God,' and the Jehovah's Witnesses may reply, 'No, He is simply a god.'

I often say, 'Did you come up with that answer as a result of your own personal investigation, research and study? Do you know Greek or did someone just inform you that this is what the verse says?' They usually say, 'Well, I was trained that way.' Usually I reply, 'I'd encourage you to reconsider what you have been told because it is inconsistent with the entire New Testament account of who Jesus really is. Scholars throughout the world cite that the Word was not "a god" but "God" and His name is Jesus Christ. His deity is central to Christianity and your eternal destiny.' Be careful on this one!

When you talk with cultists do not let them either arouse your anger or manipulate you. Be in control of the conversation. The bottom line is this: 'Jesus is God.' If you can encourage them to question and investigate their belief about this, so much the better. Some people

▓ To consider

When speaking to a Jehovah's Witness, ask him if he worships Jesus. Point out individuals who did (Matt. 14:33; 28:9,17; Luke 24:52; John 9:38). In each case, the same Greek verb is used for the word 'worship'. God wants us to worship Him in this way (John 4:23,24). By receiving exactly the same worship from men as God requires, Jesus is declaring Himself to be God.

▓ To meditate on

God wants you to be sure of Jesus. 'But about the Son he says, "Your throne, O God, will last for ever and ever, and righteousness will be the sceptre of your kingdom"' (Heb. 1:8). 'We wait for the blessed hope — the glorious appearing of our great God and Saviour, Jesus Christ' (Titus 2:13). 'The miracles I do in my Father's name speak for me ... I and the Father are one' (John 10:25b,30).

say that other great religious leaders claimed to be God. 'Buddah was God,' they say. But Buddha never made out that he was divine. He was simply deified by some after his death. In fact some of his last words were, 'I have sought for truth all my life and still haven't found it.'

People sometimes say, 'Jesus never claimed to be God.' But this is untrue. He repeatedly affirmed it. God said to Moses, '... say to the Israelites: "I AM has sent me to you"' (Exod. 3:14b). Jesus picked up the 'I am' phrase and stated, 'I tell you the truth ... before Abraham was born, I am!' (John 8:58). He also said, 'I am the way', 'I am the good shepherd', 'I am the door.' The signal was abundantly clear.

Thomas eventually realised who Jesus was. When Christ appeared to him he declared, 'My Lord and my God!' (John 20:28). The Old Testament forbade the worship of man but Jesus did not reply, 'Stop that! I'm not God.' He received the worship.

Jesus not only claimed to be God, He underlined that claim by His life. He was completely sinless, possessed amazing wisdom and performed incredible miracles. He was and is the Lord of all.

➤ Role-play.

➤ Memorise Scripture.

▓ To read

A woman, formerly a Jehovah's Witness, reported that while a Witness she encountered three types of responses. Some slammed the door in her face. These people made her feel good, since this was construed to be persecution for the sake of her faith. A second group argued heatedly and belligerently, which strengthened her convictions, since she had ready answers for their arguments. A third group gave her a personal testimony of their faith in Christ. These made the most lasting impression on her. She would reflect on what they had said. *J. Oswald Sanders*

A man who was merely a man and said the sort of things Jesus said would not be a great moral teacher. He would either be a lunatic ... or else He would be the Devil of Hell. You must make your choice ... You can shut Him up for a fool, you can spit at Him and kill Him as a demon, or you can fall at His feet and call Him Lord and God.
C. S. Lewis

'Church = Hypocrites!'

'Woe to you, teachers
of the law and
Pharisees, you
hypocrites!'
(Matt. 23:27a)

Jesus went throughout
Galilee, teaching in
their synagogues,
preaching the good
news of the kingdom,
and healing every
disease and sickness
among the people
(Matt. 4:23).

Unfortunately this observation may be all
too true. The so-called church often is full
of hypocrites (Greek — 'play-actors'). They
curse and swear during the week and hold
office in the church on Sundays.

Disarm your questioner by agreeing that
there are plenty of religious hypocrites. You
yourself may have stayed away from the church
for just that reason. But point out that
Christianity doesn't rest on the hypocrites. It is
based on the reality of Jesus Christ whose
strongest criticism was actually directed at the
religious hypocrites of His day.

When the Pharisees wanted to know whether
they should pay taxes to Caesar or not, Jesus
said, 'You hypocrites, why are you trying to trap
me?' (Matt. 22:18). But although He hated the
phoncy religious people, He loved those who
genuinely sought Him. He helped the poor and
oppressed and healed the sick. He was no play-
actor. He lived what He preached. Encourage
your questioner to focus not on those who
claim to follow Jesus but on Jesus Himself.

Closely linked with the question concerning
hypocrites is another question, namely, 'Can't I
get to heaven by being good?' People are often

▓ To consider

Read Matthew 23:28.
If Jesus were to come into your room,
could you look Him in the eye and tell
Him that you are not being hypocritical
in any of the following areas?
    gossip, use of finance, deceit, envy,
    prejudice, grudges, lust, idolatry,
    greed, honouring your parents,
    swearing, stealing, lying.
If God is challenging you about any of
these things, put it right.

▓ To meditate on

God wants you to be holy.
'People will be lovers of themselves ...
having a form of godliness but denying
its power' (2 Tim. 3:2a,5a).
'Why do you look at the speck of
sawdust in your brother's eye and pay
no attention to the plank in your own
eye?' (Matt. 7:3)
'A man is not justified by observing the
law, but by faith in Jesus Christ' (Gal.
2:16a).

hypocrites simply because they do not understand what a Christian is. They attend meetings, live reasonably moral lives, do their best to please God and assume that they are Christians.

Tell your questioner that as far as good works go, some people are better than others. His grannie would win a 'good person contest' if the other competitors were people like Adolf Hitler or Charles Manson. The problem is that God's standard is not goodness; it's perfection.

The Bible says that ' there is no-one who does good, not even one' (Ps. 14:3), and that 'all our righteous acts are like filthy rags' (Isa. 64:6). We cannot qualify on our own merits because we always fall short of God's standard. Indeed, if we could save ourselves, there would be no need for a Saviour. We are helpless unless God steps in.

God has stepped in! We read, 'the Father has sent his Son to be the Saviour of the world' (1 John 4:14b). Jesus is the only person who satisfies God's standard. He is 'a lamb without blemish or defect' (1 Pet. 1:19b), and 'by one sacrifice he has made perfect for ever those who are being made holy' (Heb. 10:14).

> Role-play.

> Memorise Scripture.

▨ To pray

Pray for churchmen and church-goers who do not have a personal relationship with Jesus Christ:

- that God will bring them into contact with Christians who will challenge their beliefs
- that God will open their hearts to receive Jesus.

Integrity is the glue that holds our way of life together. What our young people want to see in their elders is integrity, honesty, truthfulness, and faith. What they hate most of all is hypocrisy and phoniness.
Billy Graham

❏ STUDY 29

Evangelism is a process

I planted the seed, Apollos watered it, but God made it grow (1 Cor. 3:6).

'A man scatters seed on the ground. Night and day, whether he sleeps or gets up, the seed sprouts and grows, though he does not know how' (Mark 4:26b,27).

Many Christians feel discouraged when they share the gospel with someone who refuses to accept it. 'He rejected me,' they say. 'I've failed.' And the devil whispers, 'Quit. You're useless at this.' But the truth is that they haven't been rejected, Jesus has. They've just been faithful.

God has called us to evangelise — to share the good news. He does not want us to feel oppressively burdened for souls. He wants to release us to evangelise and to leave the results to Him. So there's no reason for us to become down-hearted when people refuse to repent.

The seed that we and others sow may take many weeks or even years to germinate.

It has been said that the average Christian convert needs seven different exposures to the gospel before he makes a decision for Christ. When you are talking to someone about Jesus you don't know where you are in that process. Your chief concern, therefore, is to focus not on the apparent lack of results but on the faithfulness of God — and to continue to spread the good news.

When my neighbours were expecting a baby my wife, Doris, and I did some practical things

---

▓ To do

Consider one unbelieving household in your neighbourhood.

What could you do for them this week (e.g. buy or make a cake for them, invite them for coffee/a meal, look after their children, etc.)?

Once you've decided on something, go and do it.

▓ To meditate on

God wants you to be faithful.
'Preach the Word; be prepared in season and out of season; correct, rebuke and encourage — with great patience and careful instruction' (2 Tim. 4:2).
'See how the farmer waits for the land to yield its valuable crop and how patient he is for the autumn and spring rains' (James 5:7b).

or them. On several occasions we were able to share about Jesus, but there was no response. Then one day the husband came over to our house. He told us that he and his wife had been watching someone preaching the gospel on television and that both of them had committed their lives to Jesus Christ.

I didn't think, 'Darn it! I should have got the credit!' I just rejoiced that I'd been privileged to sow, that the preacher had watered and that God had given the growth.

A girl once spoke to me after I'd been preaching at a meeting. She said, 'About eight years ago I was living with a guy, drinking and taking drugs. My life was disintegrating. Then you talked to me about Jesus Christ. I was so spaced out I think I snickered at what you shared. But last week I was saved, yesterday I was baptised and tonight they're going to pray for me to receive the baptism of the Holy Spirit. I just wanted to thank you that eight years ago you were willing to plant a seed for Jesus in my heart.'

When that happens, sharing the gospel suddenly seems so worthwhile.

▓ Food for thought

➤ Are you waiting for God to intervene in your situation?

➤ Look up the following references and write down anything that God is saying to you: Ps. 27:14; 33:20; 37:7,34; 40:1; Prov. 20:22; Isa. 30:18; 40:31; 64:4; Lam. 3:26; Mic. 7:7.

_____

_____

_____

▓ To consider

Are you in the habit of not finishing tasks because you don't have the patience to see them through (e.g. mending something, filling in official documents, cataloguing your tape collection, etc.)? Write down any uncompleted projects in a notebook.

Finish them.

Work at being patient with yourself and others.

The faith of Christ offers no buttons to push for quick service. The new order must wait for the Lord's own time, and that is too much for the man in a hurry. He just gives up and becomes interested in something else.
A. W. Tozer

Lift up your eyes

'I will make you into a great nation and I will bless you; I will make your name great, and you will be a blessing ... and all peoples on earth will be blessed through you' (Gen. 12:2,3).

The LORD said to Abram ... 'Lift up your eyes from where you are and look north and south, east and west. All the land that you see I will give to you and your offspring for ever' (Gen. 13:14,15).

I looked and there before me was a great multitude that no-one could count, from every nation, tribe, people and language, standing before the throne and in front of the Lamb (Rev. 7:9).

The Great Commission was not given in splendid isolation. It was not a sudden last minute idea. Rather, it was established in God' purposes from the beginning. It was always God's intention to reach the nations.

So when Jesus commanded His disciples to go to the ends of the earth, He was simply restating the vision that had been in God's heart all along.

Jesus lived with world vision. His Father had said to Him, 'I will ... make you a light for the Gentiles, that you may bring my salvation to the ends of the earth' (Isa. 49:6b). His mission was grounded in the Abrahamic Covenant. That's why He could say to His opposers, 'Your father Abraham rejoiced at the thought of seeing my day; he saw it and was glad' (John 8:56).

The disciples lived with world vision. In his first sermon after Pentecost Peter quoted God's promise to Abraham, 'Through your offspring all peoples on earth will be blessed' (Acts 3:25b). Paul likewise embraced the same glorious purpose of God, mentioning the unbreakable connection with Abraham five times in his letter to the Galatians alone.

▦ To consider

How should a local church express a worldwide vision (e.g. outreach, preaching — not just about church restoration)?

_____

How could you express a greater concern for the spread of the gospel to the nations (e.g. start up a prayer group for a particular country)?

_____

▦ To meditate on

God wants you to have a big vision.
'And all mankind will see God's salvation' (Luke 3:6).
'Of the increase of his government and peace there will be no end' (Isa. 9:7a).
'And this gospel of the kingdom will be preached in the whole world as a testimony to all nations, and then the end will come' (Matt. 24:14).

The early Christians lived with world vision. From the start they knew that they were involved in a far greater mission than existed on their front doorstep. Burning in their hearts was a passion to reach the nations for Jesus, so they zealously evangelised their fellow Jews and when persecution came, they reached out to the Gentiles as well (Acts 8:1–5).

God's eternal purpose has not changed. It's just that many Christians don't see it. God told Abraham to lift up his eyes and look. John looked and saw heaven populated by people from every nation.

Today, God is calling us to catch the same vision. Have you caught it?

The last words that Jesus said were, '... to the ends of the earth' (Acts 1:8). They must have rung in the disciples' ears as they made their way back to Jerusalem.

What words ring in your ears? Do you hear Jesus saying to you, 'You're just an individual that I've called to do a little thing in this corner?' Or do you hear Him declaring to you, 'You're part of a great army that I'm raising up and mobilising to reach the world?'

➢ Throughout history God's purpose has been to have a bride for His Son from every people on earth.

➢ Look up the following Scriptures which reflect this glorious goal: Ps. 2:7–9; 22:22–31; 86:9; Isa. 2:1–5; 52:7–10; Hag. 2:7; Gal. 3:8; Rev. 5:9,10.

▓ To pray

Pray for the worldwide spread of the gospel, and for the conversion of many people — particularly of those in influential positions.

Ask God to meet the spiritual, emotional and physical needs of believers who are:

• in places where there have been recent disasters
• in countries which tend to be hostile to the Christian message
• in prison for their faith
• preparing to go out on the mission field
• known to you and working abroad.

We must vigorously resist any tendencies to simply be local churches existing for internal, short-term, domestic needs. Never settle for this! God's purpose according to Psalm 2:7–9 is to give the *nations* to His Son and the local church plays a key role in this worldwide objective.
Terry Virgo
People of Destiny Magazine,
September/October 1986

☐ STUDY 31

Anyone, then, who knows the good he ought to do and doesn't do it, sins (James 4:17).

Over to you

There's a battle going on for the souls of men and women. Never has it raged more fiercely than it does today. But never have people been more open to the gospel. They cannot see it written by God's hand in the heavens, neither can they read it on the leaves of the trees. They're dependent on you and me.

God has entrusted us with the answer to the greatest need of man. He has given us the words of eternal life.

Someone once said, 'All that's required for the triumph of evil is for good men to do nothing.' Compare the stories of Jim and Tony. Jim is unemployed. One day he comes home and there's no food for his family. The children are crying with hunger and rather than see them starve, he steals a loaf of bread from a nearby store.

Tony, on the other hand, is a successful businessman. He wears expensive clothes and always looks immaculate. Late one evening he's walking home across a bridge when he hears a scream for help. He looks down in the water and sees a girl struggling for her life. Immediately he thinks, 'Oh I wish somebody were around to help her. I can't do anything

▓ To recap

Look back over this book and write down in a notebook any assignments that you have been meaning to do but haven't yet done (e.g. writing your personal tract, witnessing to a certain person, role-playing the 'objections to the gospel', etc.).

Plan now exactly when you're going to do these things — and do them.

▓ To meditate on

God wants you to fulfil your commission and speak boldly for Him.
'"Do not say, 'I am only a child.' You must go to everyone I send you to and say whatever I command you. Do not be afraid of them, for I am with you and will rescue you," declares the LORD' (Jer. 1:7,8).
'The LORD is with me; he is my helper. I will look in triumph on my enemies' (Ps. 118:7).